sunset beach dances

sunset beach dances

The Infinite Rhythms of a North Carolina Seashore

poems and photographs
by Sheree K. Nielsen

SHANTI ARTS PUBLISHING
BRUNSWICK, MAINE

Published by Shanti Arts Publishing

Cover image by Frankie Borden captured on Sunset Beach,
North Carolina. *Freestyle* and *Life Dance* photographs are
by Frankie Borden; all other photographs are by Sheree K.
Nielsen. Photographs used with permission of the artist.

Interior and cover design by Shanti Arts Designs

Shanti Arts LLC
193 Hillside Road
Brunswick, Maine 04011

www.shantiarts.com

Printed in the United States of America

ISBN: 978-1-956056-99-0 (softcover)

Library of Congress Control Number: 2023943060

For my dog children, Sabrina and Bordeaux, who spent
countless vacations on Sunset Beach (and many other
beaches across the United States), making friends, splashing
in the water, and loving the unbridled wind in their fur.
I will love and miss you forever.
You brought joy and happiness to everyone you met.

Contents

Introduction

Exploring beach towns in North Carolina in 2010, my husband and I happened upon Sunset Beach quite by accident.

Our first visit was during a torrential downpour. Grabbing our umbrellas from the car for shelter, we passed through a wooden gazebo and walked the main beach access boardwalk to the soft wet sand. The waves were tempestuous, and the wind was wild. And I was drawn to this place. We vowed to return to Sunset Beach in a few days, when the forecast was sunny.

As our visit drew to a close, we mapped a course past Sunset Beach on the way out of town. Steering our car into a parking space, we stopped at the same lot with the cute gazebo. Hand in hand, we strolled the zig-zaggy boardwalk to the beach.

Minutes after stepping foot on the soothing sand, a young boy dressed in a blue t-shirt and white board shorts surprised me by drenching me with a bucket of water. I felt like scolding him, but all I could do was chuckle. Motioning for us to follow him, the boy led us under the weathered pier, where a thirty-something woman—seated in a red webbed chair, legs crossed, reading a book—greeted me.

"That's my boy!"

"He sure has a good arm," I said.

The brown-haired woman laughed. "Where you from?"

"Missouri."

"You been to the Kindred Spirit Bench?"

"Nope," I answered, shaking my head from side to side.

The woman explained that the Kindred Spirit Bench sat high atop dunes on Bird Island—a thirty-five-minute walk due west from the last beach access at 40th Street along the shoreline.

"About forty-five years ago, someone who wished to remain anonymous built the Kindred Spirit Bench. Adjacent to the bench stood a mailbox filled with journals containing notes and letters from visitors all over the world. The journals, collected each week by 'helpers,' ensured the penned thoughts made their way back to the secret originator."

"Sitting on the bench," she said, "is the best view of Bird Island."

After our visit to Sunset Beach, I conjured images of Bird Island in my head. Obsessed with planning a visit to the Kindred Spirit Bench, upon returning home I booked a quaint vacation cottage. One month later, my blue-eyed Australian shepherd, my silver-haired handsome hubby, and I drove fifteen hours to our southern destination on a mission of self-discovery.

Over the last twelve years, there have been many more visits to Sunset Beach with my spouse and sweet fur babies. I've experienced the chilly air of March, the sun-kissed month of May, the salty sea sprays of September, and the Halloween-hued sunsets of October on the beach.

Visits to the Kindred Spirit Bench came to be a necessity, soaking in the sights and sounds of seagulls soaring overhead, driftwood washed ashore, and children building sandcastles. The rest of our days were spent lazing under our beach umbrellas—one for us, one for the canine kids. Strolling with the pups along the shoreline while looking for seashells was a daily adventure.

The pups stayed in the shallows; running away from waves as they came crashing ashore, they were too chicken to get anything but their hind quarters wet while splashing in the warm ocean. The hubster usually read a book, while I people-watched and restrained the pooches—all the while whimpering—when other dogs strutted past.

I'm guided by an unexplainable urge that draws me to this resplendent place. I love the east-west beach with magnificent sunrises and sunsets, the iconic pier, the sleepy town feel of the island, and especially, the people and the dogs.

I find comfort and solace walking the beach, healed from all the hardships in my life. The last five years were really rough—chemo treatments (twice for my lymphoma), severe depression, the loss of three fur babies, and the passing of loved ones.

So, in honor of all the hard times, and definitely the good, I dance on the beach at sunset the night before we head home. Hubby finds a jazz station on his phone that serves as the background music for me, and I get my best groove on. (He usually records my excellent moves!)

I hope Sunset Beach Dances, its poetry and photography, transport you back to your favorite beach, no matter where you are, no matter your worries. And if you dance a little, that's okay too!

I wish you peace, love, and sea shells.

Sheree

WANDER

Adagio

Gambol with me across
scintillating velveteen shores.

With effervescence,
spin me,
with gentle precision,
lift my nubile body.

The sea commands my hidden desires,

Golden Sunset Dance

My heart lies with the sea
on a sailing boat
barefoot,
hiking windward.
The warmth of ropes between
soft, yet sinewy hands...

Golden sunshine
bathes the nape of my neck.

Waves rocks me like a lullaby
into slumber.

The seagulls raw 'meh' entices
in the foggy morning
with bubbling enthusiasm
welcoming the ocean
in my soul.

Surfer's Dance

A lissome figure
in neoprene wetsuit
rests at the shoreline of life
pondering thoughts...

Perhaps she'll ride the beach break,
Sailing safely and smoothly
on a wave
moving over a shallow sea bed alive
with marine life.

Or perhaps she'll search for a
reef break
with ebbs and flow,
and tempestuous uncertainty
morphing into the
perfect wave
and the ride
of a lifetime.

Which will she choose?

Botecito

Small boat
tell me of escapades and your life
story.

White ibis at sunrise,
oystermen hunting at low tide,
trips to deserted islands,
lover's stolen strawberry champagne kisses.

Rock me in your acquiescence.

Oh, the places you have seen...

Umbrella Dance

A rainbow canvas hides two lovers,
stealing kisses and whispering sweet nothings.

The charcoal gray sea shore
caresses naked toes
in a gritty embrace.

The Reel

Studying the sea,
anglers, cast rods—one up, one down,
masterfully, skillfully, calculating with
accuracy
the exact moment the tarpon or grouper
will tease their filament.

Just a couple of
barefoot, blue-jeaned,
silver-haired foxes.

Line Dancing

Rigid lines intersect,
imbricate
like roads on a map,
lead us on
adventures to locations
unfamiliar.

Silhouettes dance
against saffron and aubergine-hued
skies
posing reflections on tepid waters.

Wanderers
all are we…
on a journey of finding hope
and self-discovery.

Bicycle Roundel

Miles she's pedaled her trusty bike
with fat tires hugging the sand.

The tan leather seat and the grip of the handlebars
feel good to the touch
as she speeds up the beach access
to her next destination.

She reposes
astride the marsh.

The sky paints lavender and dreamsicle strokes
as the sun gently pulls a blanket of rest
on dune grasses.

The Swing

Resembling a pea in a pod,
she sleeps.

Oblivious to their presence,
beachgoers wander the seashore at low tide
searching for keyhole sand dollars,
Scotch bonnets and lighting whelks…

Others pass nearby under the pier.
She breathes soft and low, swinging in
a mesh security blanket.

The wind taps her shoulder with a
gentle breeze, as wave crests
break in the distance.

Still, she sleeps.

The Shuffle

We're all just
visitors
on a temporary vacation
meandering along
the sand
doing the best
we can.

Not knowing which
chance
meeting on the beach
will blossom into
a lifelong friendship,
or random tide washes treasures
ashore to discover
and love.

Maybe a fishing adventure
will yield an abundant
catch of crustaceans?

But we're doing the best we can
just shuffling along...

CONTEMPLATE

Step Dance

Abandoned by a storm,
a set of "no trespassing steps"
reside on the east end—
formerly a beacon of privacy to
someone's
home.

Flat on the sand, they lead
to nowhere.

But tilt the horizon,
and the possibilities are
endless.

Kindred Spirit Dance

Slipping off his leather sandals, he selects
one of the tattered notebooks
housed inside the ebony mailbox.

Reposed on the weathered bench,
he studies
Old Glory, penning thoughts
in the worn journal.

"Wil, you would have loved this spot . . . "

Moon Dance

Heavenly moon shine down,
guide me through the darkness
as I perambulate the lustrous
seashore, imbibing in your
sweet nectar.

What shall I make of this gravitational
attraction between you and earth…
the ebb and flow of the tides?

Beach Dance

We're all born strong and unblemished,
similar to a perfect scallop shell before it begins
its journey with the sea.

The shell, carried lovingly
through the ocean, moves with each
wave, picking up the sand
and the grit
before landing in the shallows
or a sandy shoreline.
Smoothed by the tides...

After life's storms, I yearn for the beach
just like the scallop.

I seek comfort and solace in the sand.
Meandering, the gritty substance fills up
the space between my toes,
equal to precious time healing
the holes
in my past—
chemotherapy, depression,
the loss of a dog...

My time at the beach is my own.
No one can steal it away.
A safe place to explore, dream,
smile, wander, admire,
reflect.

No matter the steps I've ambled, I feel
motionless.

I eye the weathered pier in the distance.
Ruminating on the far-reaching journey
of today...

I love how the beach always smells like
coconut and salty sea sprays.

The beach renews
the soul and imagination.

I soak it all in.
I pause, breathe, and survey
the dunes, the sea,
the sand.

Life Dance

The tides wash clean
imperfections, hardships and
sins
of a lifetime,
as the simple grains of sand
settle in empty crevices
called 'experience'
and transform rough
beginnings
into smooth.

Jimmy's Dance

A veteran's cigar-hued face shows age
behind cool aviator glasses
and a neatly trimmed silver
goatee.

Intently, he peruses the newspaper
keeping an ever-watchful eye
on the rod tip
across the pier.

Deep inside he pushes down
smoldering secrets
of the Vung Tau region.

Reflective Dance

Elusive as the tides
causing
waves to ripple
to shore,
such are the shadows
cast by reflections
of our thoughts
capturing youthfulness.

We find solace
and strength in the water
creating such impressions.

All we need do is reflect.

The Stroll

At day's end,
In quiet formation,
Silhouettes stroll the greige wooden planks.

One by one,
gear and coastered coolers in tow.

Timeless hours spent
Reflecting, ruminating, casting…

FREE

Allegro

Bring me your joy
and I will increase it
fourfold.

Show me your love and I will
calm your heart with my
wings.

Soaring briskly above wisteria skies,
my life is fragrant when
you're nearby.

Free Dance

Looking skyward,
I felt the weight of the world lift beneath my wings.

I dipped and soared,
crossing paths with similar creatures
for mere
seconds.

The turquoise sea
ambles between the horizon and offing.

I celebrate exhilaration.

Freedom Dance

Resting quietly on the sandy shore,
cool water rushes soft paw pads as
Red Dog memorizes movement passing
through his vision...
children splashing, bicyclists peddling,
sand castle artists creating, moms with floppy straw hats reading,
the sleek golden retriever carrying a plastic water bottle,
seagulls and pelicans dancing
to the rhythm of the sea.

There's freedom in his eyes,
happiness in an upturned flew,
contentment in his soul...
rescued by a family
who just couldn't resist
big, sloppy,
canine kisses.

Universal Peace Dance

Give me a world
free from conflict,
one of harmony and kindness,
where love prevails in the face of
adversity.

Where the sanderlings mellifluous song echoes
amid champagne
and indigo blue sunsets...

Where glistening summery shorelines
become eye candy for miles...

Where people speak to inspire...

Where hatred
is not
a word...

Free Style

Crank up the music,
move your body,
move your body.

Making shadows
in the sand,
it's been a while since
I free-styled,
longing to be wild.

THE ISLAND

Criss Cross

A simple handmade cross
of twigs and twine
sits atop the dune.

Many have photographed,
many more have passed,
and some have prayed
near this sacred place
blessed by God's grace.

Dance of the Heart

The island slumbers
in tranquility
as a blood orange
sunset cloaks
the heart-shaped marsh.

Flower Dance

Although I have shallow roots,
happiness blankets the ground wherever
I reside.

Delicately aged petals lilt in the wind,
contemplating
a new season
to bloom.

Purple Haze

Last evening
the sky's hues of fire pink,
lavender and powderpuff blue
slipped into the time before night,
and the ocean's shimmer felt like a warm summer slumber
in the company of the rustic pier and the charcoal-hued pilings.

Marsh Dance

Muted sunlight permeates
thousands of reeds and marsh grasses
peeking through chambre' waters
of wetland
enticing eager kayakers
to glide like glass
in her embrace with
dreams of discovering unexpected
pleasures
around each
bend.

Sand Castle Dance

Castles in the sand
lovingly carved by
young men clad in white shirts,
and board shorts,
tossing back wavy black
locks.

Intricate ethereal designs
represent dreams of a medieval
times,
of brave knights and foot
soldiers,
brought to life.

The Boardwalk

One pale foot in front of the other
I march at a brisk pace
to the dance
the beach access sings,
edging me closer
to the sea.

With tattered book, bottled water,
and sleek sunglasses
in hand,
husband follows in tow with beach cart,
umbrella and chairs.

Anticipation peaks as I step gingerly
as the powdery granules
and lure of Sunset Beach
beckons.

After a nap, people-watching, a somewhat tan,
and windblown hair,
I saunter the promenade
to the beach house.

Of course, husband is
in tow with the
heavy stuff.

Tidepool Boogie

Beams of lemon-white
cast mirrored reflections
on weathered pier pilings
at sunset.

Shadowed tidepools swirl,
imitate, encompass life—

Baby crabs, barnacles and sea
stars scatter, seek
refuge in the shallow
sustenance.

FUREVER FRIENDS

Best Friend's Dance

The two figures saunter
side-by-side
sinking toes and paws
deep in the chilly sand,
stepping briskly.

What treasures will they find along
their journey?

Sticks to be chased
Crabs to be sniffed
Sand castles to be built
Sunsets to be enjoyed
Friends to be made

Just two buddies
with parallel lives
totally in sync.
Best friends forever.

Bordeaux's Dance

strolling the seashore
dune grasses wavering
memories of Red Dog
scampering in the sand

Emmy's Dance

Her snout—
graced by whitish-beige whiskers.

Big brown eyes
round out her sweet face.

Beach girl frolics in the cool
Atlantic
locating, parading treasures
in need of recovery.

Drenched in beads of salty sea
the island is her liquid playground.

Welcoming canine friends
at water's edge.

Sea Dog Dance

In reverence, I bow
my head. I listen to
my animal child
panting next to me
and the melody of waves
crashing.

Lifting my head,
my eyes caress the offing.

I inhale, then exhale,
slow deliberate
breaths.
Salty sea air teases
lips and nostrils.

Daddy's Dance

Leisurely,
we trek beside the sea shore.

I, with my wiggly, jiggly derrière,
prance, trying to keep pace
with Daddy's long strides.

We wet our paws and feet in the soothing water,
tiptoe around darting sand crabs,
dig for seashells,
side-step gingerly,
and parade my beauty for all to see.

And of course,
dance with Daddy.

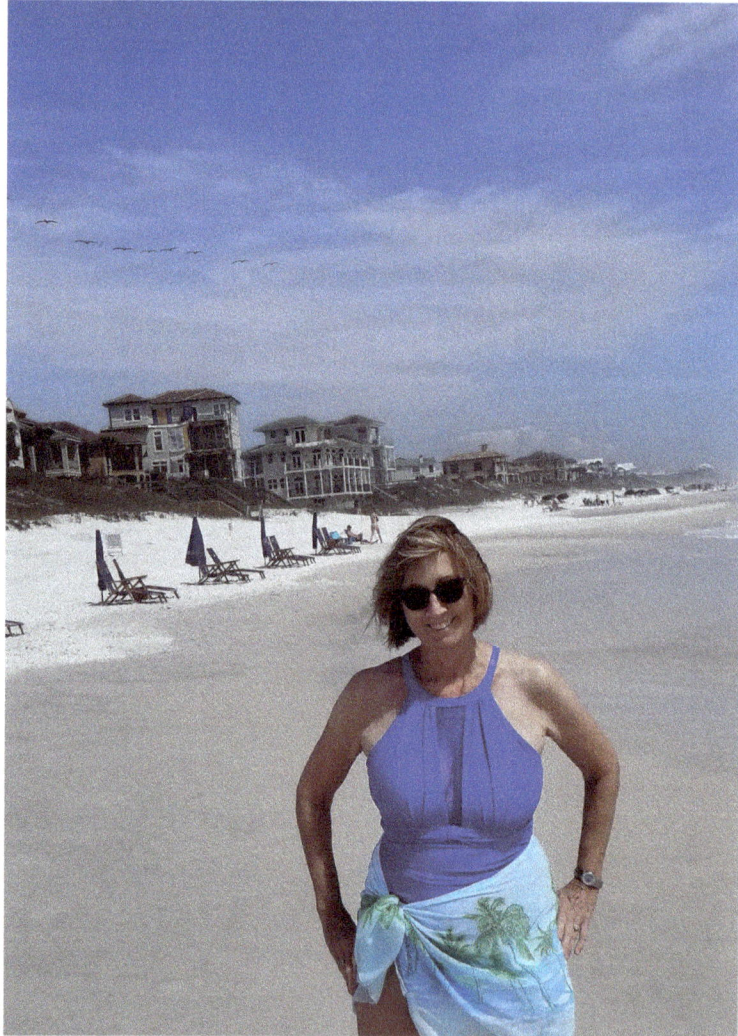

SHEREE K. NIELSEN believes that every picture tells a story, combining her love of photography and writing with colorful visual descriptions and healing messages found in her coffee table books, essay collections, and children's books. She finds inspiration in travel, nature, family, and pets. As a two-time survivor of Waldenstrom's macroglobulinemia lymphoma, she believes in cherishing every moment of life.

Sheree is author/photographer/poet of 2021 Royal Dragonfly Book Award Winner *Coffee Coma*, poems and photographs about our love affair and life with coffee, having received First Place in Photography/Fine Art and Honorable Mention in Poetry. A 2019 Royal Dragonfly Book Award Winner, *Mondays In October*, love songs for the beach, received First Place in Poetry, Fine Art/Photography and Honorable Mention for Coffee Table Books.

Other books include the 2015 Da Vinci Eye Award Winner *Folly Beach Dances*, inspired by the sea and her lymphoma journey; the 2019 Chanticleer Little Peeps First Place Category Winner and Montaigne Medal Finalist *Midnight The One-Eyed Cat*, a picture book; and the 2019 Chanticleer Finalist *Ocean Rhythms Kindred Spirits: An Emerson-Inspired Essay Collection on Travel, Nature, Family and Pets*. Her other works are well represented in travel magazines and publications.

When not writing, she's discovering new beaches and cafes with her patient husband. Four content cats complete her family.

Connect with Sheree at shereenielsen.wordpress.com.

Shrimp Dance

Crustaceans dance for dinner.
antennae whip,
bodies sway to the ocean's song,
attracting prey.

Only to be caught by fisherman . . .

Flaming red opaque shell
attracts.
Morsels on circular ceramic
trays,
dipped into tomato-red
cocktail sauce.

Over the lips you go.
pure white meat, so savory
to the taste.

Honk if you love shrimp!

OPEN

OPEN

HONK
IF YOU
LOVE
SHRIMP

SHANTI ARTS

NATURE ▪ ART ▪ SPIRIT

Please visit us online
to browse our entire book catalog,
including poetry collections and fiction,
books on travel, nature, healing, art,
photography, and more.

Also take a look at our highly regarded art
and literary journal, *Still Point Arts Quarterly*,
which may be downloaded for free.

www.shantiarts.com

Also by Sheree K. Nielsen
and published by SHANTI ARTS:

Mondays in October

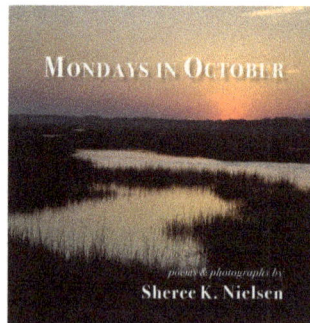

Coffee Coma

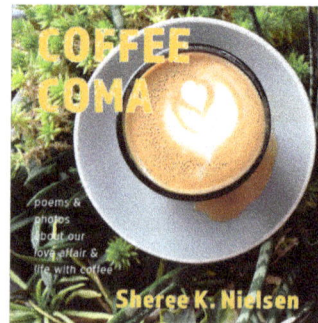

www.ingramcontent.com/pod-product-compliance
Lightning Source LLC
Chambersburg PA
CBHW041120280326
41928CB00061B/3472